How to Use a Compass for Kids

Mastering Land Navigation with Exciting Games and Activities

Table of Contents

Introduction

How to Use a Compass for Kids is a timeless and efficient book that will help every kid master land navigation. This book serves as a compass rose to guide children through unknown paths and a crowded world. All these can be achieved with compelling activities, historical facts, and engaging games. The sole aim is to educate and empower young minds with fundamental knowledge on how to use a compass while encouraging the need for this skill for outdoor exploration and adventure. Through hands-on experiences, children will not only learn the practical applications of a compass but also develop crucial problem-solving and critical-thinking skills.

With *"How to Use a Compass for Kids,"* children are not just learning about cardinal directions, azimuths, and orienteering techniques. They are embarking on exciting scavenger hunts, creating their own compasses, and participating in interactive activities designed to sharpen their navigation skills. This book provides immersive storytelling and captivating illustrations, taking children on a journey across landscapes, both real and imagined.

What truly sets this book apart is its emphasis on experiential learning. It doesn't just present educational content, it transforms the field of navigation into an exciting adventure for kids. It also encourages children to understand that amidst a busy world, there's a path set out just for them. This unique approach makes learning about navigation not only educational but also fun and engaging.

So rest assured that your kid will have a great time learning and mind-building. They will embark on virtual expeditions to distant lands, solving puzzles and overcoming obstacles along the way. With each chapter comes a discovery to ensure that knowledge and exposure are built on the previous foundation of knowledge.

Encourage your children to open their minds to learning and participate in every activity by getting involved. This will prolong the fun. Good luck!

Chapter 1: Introduction to the Compass

There are territories full of adventures that you have yet to explore because you don't know how to find your way around. This mysterious tool has the power to reveal hidden maps, unlock new paths, and set a whole new pace for your adventures.

The Earth is a giant place to live and move around; it has great width and length and cannot be fully explored by the faint-hearted. This also means that it's so big you could easily get lost in it.

1. *Before technology, people would use landmarks and the position of the stars to know where they were and where they were going. Source: https://unsplash.com/photos/silhouette-photography-of-person-oMpAz-DN-9I*

However, thanks to technology, you have GPS to help you stay on track, but it wasn't always like this. In the beginning, there was something called a sense of compassing - People were forced to rely on things like the positions of the stars, the direction of the wind, landmarks, and rudimentary maps to find their way around. All these took place before the invention of the compass device in 200 BC, and since then, everything has changed!

In this chapter, you will explore the possibilities of the compass device, its origins, its inner workings, the secret behind its ability to navigate through the most intertwined path, and games and activities to help you fully understand its use. Prepare yourself, for this journey will test your courage, challenge your intellect, and spark your curiosity about the world around you.

Compasses and Their Importance in Navigation

Have you ever come across a toy compass or used an actual one with your friends? As much as a compass helps the big guys who run the ships, it can also be used for fun on your everyday outdoor explorations.

How can you recognize a compass when you see one? Simple. A compass is usually labeled with the four cardinal points: North, South, East, and West. Most times, these labels come with just the initials N, S, E, and W.

Then, there is also a magnetic needle that is always fixed on the point labeled North. Using this, you can interpret the direction of the other points as East being on the right hand of North, West being on the left, and South being on the opposite side.

Compasses are valuable because they've played a big role in creating the world map. A map shows the tiniest of details in places like street corners, landmarks, river lines, underground pipelines, and so on. Without compasses, there would be no maps and no means to navigate paths.

2. *A compass is a small but useful tool that looks similar to a watch and helps you find directions. Source: https://unsplash.com/photos/person-holding-black-and-green-compass-pointing-to-west-3jBU9TbKW7o*

Initially, compasses were mostly used by sailors while they were out on the sea. You see, out there in the sea, it isn't easy to discover landmarks that help sailors navigate. This becomes even more difficult when it gets cloudy and sudden unpredictable storms and waves set in. All these made things difficult at a time when people were heavily dependent on stars, most especially the North Polaris, as an aid to find their way. This is why the compass is particularly needed in sailing. Today, you can find the compass almost everywhere, including modern appliances, apps, and even DIY tools.

3. *Compasses were used at sea for sailors to navigate the open waters. Source: https://pixabay.com/id/illustrations/mengirimkan-bajak-laut-petualangan-8726521/*

How Compasses Were Discovered

Inventions happen because humans are constantly searching for ways to make tasks easier and to reduce their workload as much as possible. This has led to the most amazing discoveries in history, and so much more has yet to be discovered!

Long ago, humans began to realize that the Earth was more than just a ball of sand and water. The Earth possessed what was called the Magnetic field – a force that allowed it to pull objects to itself. Objects like iron can automatically become magnetic just by associating with a magnetic stone called Lodestone.

People also realized that the force of the Earth's magnetism causes magnets to pull toward the North or South naturally. This is why the compass is made with a magnetic lodestone needle placed on a piece of wood or other materials that allows it to spin in four directions: North, South, East, and West. As time evolved, so did the ease of using the compass. Now, compasses are labeled with more directions to make interpretation much easier.

Why You Should Learn to Use a Compass

You should learn to use a compass for the various reasons below:

- **Navigate Your Path**

With the compass, you can learn to position yourself and find directions if you ever get lost or need to find something. This will equip you with a very important skill that you just might need in the future.

- **Adventures, Games, and Fun**

When you have a compass on you, you can think of the world as a place waiting to be explored, and that tool is the key to many gateways. You can begin by learning what the four cardinal points are and how to distinguish one point from the other. More of this will be discussed in the chapters that follow, so make sure to read till the end of the book.

- **It Helps in Astronomy**

Did you know that there is something called the True North and the Magnetic North? When someone mentions the North in relation to Astronomy and Geology, keep this in mind. The True North is where the North Pole lies, and the Magnetic North is what your compass needle directs you to. The difference is that the True North is a fixed point associated with the Earth's rotation, and the magnetic North isn't fixed as it constantly pulls objects toward the south pole.

- **To Find Your Place in a Crowded World**

The world is indeed crowded with so many things and with people almost everywhere you go. This could make you feel overwhelmed, especially when you're all by yourself, so you should keep your compass handy to pull through all that. A compass does have the ability to help you both physically and metaphorically, meaning that amid all that noise, there's always a path just for you. Who knows, you also get to use this fun tool to play games like scavenger hunts and much more. Look out for games and fun activities lined up just for you in the chapters that follow!

The compass is a very special tool, and it's a key part of every adventure. With it, you can sail through the waters and climb over mountains without feeling lost. When you get to understand the various ways it works, you will be invincible. The compass is very easy to use and learn, and you will soon see why after going through the simple and fun-filled guide in this book.

Chapter 2: Understanding the Compass

The Compass comes in really handy, especially when you understand how it works. To know this, you'll need to learn its few tricks and come to terms with its parts and their functions, like the four compass points, the measurement degrees, the magnetic needle, and so on. All these will be broken down in simple and easy terms for you in this chapter.

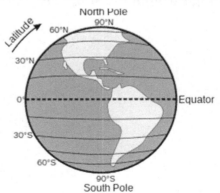

4.   The Earth is a huge magnet with two ends; the South Pole and the North Pole. Source: Djexplo, CCo, via Wikimedia Commons: https://commons.wikimedia.org/wiki/File:Latitude_of_the_Earth _fr.svg

You'd also get to enjoy lined-up activities and games to better build your understanding of the compass device.

Understanding The Parts of a Compass

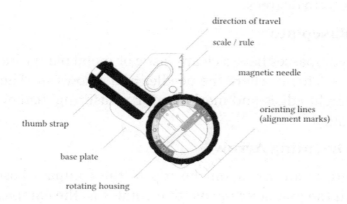

COMPASS PARTS

5.   *Components of a compass. Source: gonz4, CC0, via Wikimedia Commons: https://commons.wikimedia.org/wiki/File:Orienteering_thumb_c ompass_parts_-_en.svg*

Just like any other skill, there are basic things you need to know to develop your understanding, and the major parts are the first step for a Compass. They include:

1.   The Magnetic Needle

This needle-like object centered on the Compass is pointed like a needle. It rotates to show you the direction of the magnetic North. Like a tiny arrow, it has a red end consistently pointing toward the North and a white or black end pointing toward the south.

2. Compass Dial

The Compass has a round face, and if you look closely, you'll notice numbers marked on the surface. These numbers range from 0 to 360 degrees, and they help you measure your directions in degrees.

3. Baseplate

All compasses have a clear plastic or metal plate within the compass. This is where the needles and arrows sit. The plate has straight edges and markings for measuring distance and direction.

4. Orienting Arrow

There is an arrow on the top of the compass baseplate beneath the magnetic needle that rotates as the compass dial is turned. It's also called an orienting line, and its primary function is to align the compass with the Earth's magnetic fluid. This arrow is really effective when you try to align a compass to a map.

5. Direction of Travel Arrow

This arrow located at the end of the baseplate on the compass points towards your destination.

6. Rotating Bezel

The rotating Bezel is the ring around the compass dial that can be turned clockwise or anticlockwise. Rotating the Bezel to align with the direction of travel allows you to determine your direction by measuring the distances between locations on a map.

Major Types of Compass and Their Uses

People use compasses for different reasons, which has resulted in the creation of different types to suit unique purposes. Here are some of the major types of compasses you can find and the specific purpose for which they were created.

The Magnetic Compass

This remains the oldest existing compass in the world. Its build is different from that of modern-day electronic compasses. It has a magnetic needle that constantly aligns itself with the Earth's magnetic North.

Here are the different types:

- **Marine Compass:** This type has a magnetic needle immersed in a fluid, which makes it easy for you to read. As the name implies, it's mostly used by sailors because the magnetic needle absorbs the motions of the boat, making it stable and easy to read.

6. A console marine compass. Source: CLI, CC BY-SA 4.0 <https://creativecommons.org/licenses/by-sa/4.0>, via Wikimedia Commons. https://commons.wikimedia.org/wiki/File:MT_V.E.B._Console_Marine_Compass.jpg

- **Prismatic Compass:** This type has a glass prism or sometimes a Lens. It's sometimes also designed by combining two chemical elements, phosphorus, and tritium, which gives it a glow in the dark.

7. *Prismatic compass. Source: Remote People, CC BY-SA 4.0 <https://creativecommons.org/licenses/by-sa/4.0>, via Wikimedia Commons. https://commons.wikimedia.org/wiki/File:WWI_Compass_1918_ ER_Watts_Verner%27s_Pattern.jpg*

- **GPS:** This is a modern-day compass that uses satellites in the Earth's orbit to predict your exact location and bearing.

Gyrocompass

A gyrocompass is similar in description to a gyroscope, but they have different functions. It uses electrically powered fast-spinning wheels to find the bearing of distance and locations. It has a few advantages over the magnetic Compass, like helping to find the true North (where the Earth's rotational axis is), and they are not as susceptible to magnetic fields as the first listed compasses.

How Compasses Work

To understand how the compass works, you need to know the key functions of each part.

Identifying the Magnetic Needle

By now, you already know that the magnetic needle is highly attracted to the Earth's magnetic field. For this reason, it aligns itself with the magnetic lines of force constantly pulling toward the north pole. This is why the needle always points towards the magnetic North.

Aligning the Orienting Arrow

After identifying the magnetic needle, hold the compass on your palm and adjust the compass dial until the orienting arrow is on the same line as the magnetic needle. This simple act will align the compass with the Earth's magnetic field.

Setting Your Direction

Next, rotate the compass dial to adjust the direction-of-travel arrow towards your desired destination. This is the direction you are to head in.

Reading the Compass

Hold the compass level and read the direction-of-travel arrow. This shows the direction you need to go to reach your destination.

Using the Compass

Use the compass to navigate by keeping the direction-of-travel arrow pointing toward your destination. As you move, the magnetic needle will adjust, and you can re-align the orienting arrow to stay on course.

Using the Compass in Navigation and Outdoor Activities

You might get lost if it's your first time trying to navigate your way in an adventurous journey. Using an application or a GPS is good, but it may not be good enough in situations where you lose transmission or power. This is the essence of your Compass. As old as it may be, it remains ever-efficient in never letting you down as long as you understand how it works. Initially, it may seem complicated, but with more practice and consistency, you will soon become a professional at using it.

8. *Using the compass in your outdoor adventures will make you feel like you're on top of the world. Source: https://www.pexels.com/photo/smiling-girl-holding-an-inflatable-globe-8083738/*

Since the essence of this book is to provide you with as much basic understanding as possible of how to use a compass, below is an activity to help you get a great start on understanding your Compass.

Activities and Games

Activity 1

Compass Mining: To help you get familiar with the labeled parts of a compass in a fun and engaging way.

Materials Needed:

- Bingo cards with labeled parts of a compass (e.g., needle, direction of travel arrow, bezel, baseplate)
- Compass sketches or diagrams for reference
- Markers or chips for marking bingo squares
- Prizes for winners (optional)

Instructions:

- You can play this game with friends and families
- Show the participant a sketched compass or diagram with labeled parts as a reference.
- Provide them with a bingo card and a marker or chip to mark off their squares.
- Now begin by calling out the name of a compass part (for example, "needle," "bezel"). For anyone to describe their functions.
- The game continues until someone completes a row, column, or diagonal on their bingo card and calls out, "Bingo!"

Put your knowledge to the test by being familiar with the different parts of the compass and how they work. This chapter serves as a foundation for the next chapter, which will discuss the basics of navigation.

Get ready for real adventures when you get a handle on your compass.

Chapter 3: Getting Started with Basic Navigation

As discussed in the previous chapter, there are different kinds of compasses for different purposes. The features your compass has depend on what you want, with the most common components discussed in Chapter 2.

If you have a physical compass, you can check the components to see if it's best for your kind of adventure. This chapter teaches the basics of compass navigation, which includes learning the cardinal directions, understanding how to use or read degrees and bearings, and following up activities and games to solidify your knowledge.

9.   *Using a compass can make your adventures more interesting. Source: https://www.pexels.com/photo/a-kid-wearing-a-compass-watch-6034568/*

Learning Cardinal Directions

Cardinals are very common terms in the world today; it's often used during specific school activities, weather forecasts, adventure movies, and so on. Your cardinals are your North, South, East, and West. They help you determine your locations, understand distances and bearings on your map, find routes, and locate places around the world. Even nature helps you understand your cardinal directions. For example, the sun can be used to tell the East from the West as it always rises from the East and sets to the West. The compass is a really good way to know your cardinals, too. On the compass, you have your magnetic needle, which is always pulled towards the magnetic North and marked as 'N.' Then, you have other cardinal points highlighted for easy navigation.

How to Read Your Cardinal Directions

Now that you know what cardinal directions are, it's necessary to know how to read them using your compass. Carefully study these two images below and notice where all cardinal directions are stationed on a compass and a compass rose.

10. *The four cardinal (main) directions or points are North, West, East, and South. Source: Brosen, modification by Howcheng, CC BY 3.0 <https://creativecommons.org/licenses/by/3.0>, via Wikimedia Commons: https://commons.wikimedia.org/wiki/File:Simple_compass_rose.svg*

A compass rose is sometimes called a wind rose or a compass star. It appears like a figure on your maps, charts, and compasses as cardinal directions (N, S, E, and W) and intermediate points (NE, NW, SE, SW, and so on.)

As you look at your compass rose and your compass, you will notice that the four cardinal directions are positioned on the four main numbers of a clock. At noon, you'll see the letter N, which represents North. Just like a clock, you read your cardinals in a clockwise position. Next to N is 3 o'clock, and here you'll see E as in the East. Going further to 6 O'clock, you'll see S as in South, then 9 o'clock where you see W as in West. These are your four cardinal directions, and remember that they're always read in a clockwise direction. You can use this mnemonic to stay on track –Never Eat Soggy Waffles or NESW.

The intermediate directions come next. Just like we did before, in a clockwise position, between North and East, you'll have the abbreviation NE for Northeast. Between East and South, you'll have SE for Southeast. Then, between South and West, you'll have SW for Southwest and then NW for Northwest. These are called intermediate, intercardinal, or ordinal directions.

Why are Intermediate Directions Important?

They give you a more precise form of navigation because they let you understand in-between positions that are not directly aligned with the cardinal directions. The intermediate directions can further be broken down into 8 secondary intercardinal and then further into 16 more intermediary directions, making it a total of 32 points.

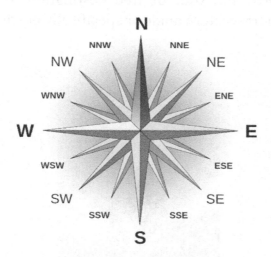

11. *Intermediate directions on a compass. Source: I, Andrew pmk, CC BY-SA 3.0 <http://creativecommons.org/licenses/by-sa/3.0/>, via Wikimedia Commons. https://commons.wikimedia.org/wiki/File:Compass_Rose_English _North.svg*

Understanding Degrees and Bearing

To find a compass bearing, you have to find the angle between N -North and where you're headed. This could be a distance to an object, a landmark, a specific spot, or a direction. A compass bearing is like a measurement of how far clockwise you have to turn from North to face a certain direction.

For example, imagine you're on a ship, and you see that it's going straight West; that means its bearing would be around 300 degrees because that's how many degrees you've turned from North to face West. Looking at the diagram of the compass above, you'll see how the degrees are stationed on the edges. 300° would specifically be WNW -West northwest. A 20° bearing can be read on your compass as the angles between North and your desired destination. It should be around the northeastern angle or specifically north-northeast.

12. To ascertain the direction of travel, extend your hands while holding the compass. Source: https://unsplash.com/photos/person-holding-compass-T57t6ZUT2Kc

Standard Compass Bearings

These include your basic cardinal directions. There are also 16 more points between them, each 22.5 degrees apart. For example, if you start North and turn 22.5 degrees clockwise (towards East), you'll be facing north-northeast, and so on, until you come back to where you started.

These are your intermediary directions. 45° after your pure directions, north, south, East, and west, you get your Northeast and southwest. Notice that the initial names always begin with the North or South, after which the East and West are attached. When a point is close to a pure direction, it's named based on the pure directions they're closest to - east-northeast or south-southwest.

Games and Activities

1. **Compass Degree Match:** To help you get familiar with the degree and bearing on a compass and how to use them.

Materials Needed:

- Compass
- Marker, highlighter, or chalk
- Pen and paper
- Timer
- Open outdoor space or large indoor area with enough room for you to move around

Instructions:

Level 1

- Use the marker or chalk to draw a large circle on the ground, representing the compass dial.

- Divide the circle into segments as seen on the image provided early in the chapter, each labeled with a compass degree (e.g., 0°, 90°, 180°, 270°).

- Now label your pure cardinal points (N, E, S, W) outside the edge of the circle.

- To hold the compass, make sure your palm is stretched out openly. You won't need it until the end of this challenge.

- Take note of each of these numbers: 45°, 135°, 225°, 315°. Write them on paper and keep them with you in the circle.

- Now, stand at the center of the compass circle and point in the direction you think these numbers fall to.

- Bring out your compass and check to confirm. Adjust your pointing direction to align with the compass's.

Level 2

- Now, set a timer, beginning with 1 minute and going downwards for each attempt you make.

- Try it out with this new set of numbers;

Activity 2

The Sun Tracking Challenge: To help you identify the direction of sunrise and sunset using good observation and critical thinking skills.

13. Make sure you have access to a somewhat clear sky so you can see the horizon. Source: https://www.pexels.com/photo/person-standing-on-sand-301952/

Materials Needed:

- Clear sky or access to an outdoor area with a clear view of the horizon

- Watch or smartphone with timekeeping capabilities

- Compass

Instructions:

- Choose a location with an unobstructed view of the horizon, like an open field or rooftop.

- Browse out the approximate times of sunrise and sunset using a weather app or website.

- Just before sunrise, take your compass out and turn towards the East. Observe the direction from which the sun rises.

- Mark this direction mentally or physically by pointing or placing a marker on the ground.

- As sunset approaches, face west and observe the direction in which the sun sets.

- Compare your observations with the predicted time gotten from that website and check for accuracy.

- You can take this further by tracking the sun's movement at different times of the day (e.g., morning, noon, evening) to gain a better understanding of its path across the sky.

- Write down your observations and try to use this knowledge during your daily activities. The more accurate, the better.

The cardinal points are essential for reading and understanding your directions better. The numbers and degrees are not enough to navigate your path. This is why in this chapter, you've learned the importance of knowing the four pure cardinal directions, their intermediate and sub-intermediary needed to navigate a compass. You've also learned to read your bearings, how you tell the east from the west and the north from the south. To solidify this knowledge, you've been given activities and games to teach you how to read your cardinals in a fast and easy way.

Chapter 4: Mastering Compass Skills

So far, you've learned the basics of understanding how a compass works (mechanism) and the words used to label them (terminologies) related to navigation using a magnetic compass.

This chapter takes you a step further to learn about advanced navigation techniques like using a compass with a map, finding bearings on maps using triangulation methods, and a lot more!

Keep your mind open, your maps close, and your compass closer.

14. The ability to interpret maps is a crucial skill that aids in effective navigation. Source: https://www.pexels.com/photo/magnifying-glass-and-wind-rose-on-maps-7412095/

Advanced Navigation Techniques

Navigation generally revolves around honing and using skills that allow you to find and unbox directions and positions.

In this book, navigation is attached to the skillful use of a magnetic compass in finding locations and understanding bearings so you can never be lost. Understanding and using these navigational techniques takes time to get the hang of. Especially for mapping, you need to be familiar with mapping terms for bearing and intersections.

Don't worry; it's not as difficult as it sounds! Let's begin:

Correcting Your Compass for Declination

Do you still remember the Magnetic North and the True North and their position in the compass?

The angle in the compass that lies between these two is called **declination**, and it's greatly affected by your current location and the constant movement of the earth. Without adjusting your compass to get the declination angle, you might end up getting lost. Getting the declination is quite simple, but you'll need your map. Most maps have declination presented in a diagram, which also comes with the date it was last updated. If you need a more accurate reading, you have to get a newer map.

15. Make sure your map is new and updated to make sure that you're exploring properly. Source: https://www.pexels.com/photo/a-compass-on-the-map-7235903/

Here's how you can recognize the declination on your map: you will notice a degree and a direction attached to a number. For example, 15° East. You don't have to worry if you have an old map, you can find an online declination calculator for your location.

If you've taken note of your declination, the next step is to do a bit of math. Get a calculator on standby to confirm the figures. If your direction is pointing west, subtract that number from your magnetic North to get your true North bearing.

To make it even easier, see this example:

Let's say you're using a compass to navigate, and it shows that you're facing West. If the declination angle on your map is 15 degrees East, you will then subtract 15 degrees from the direction your compass is pointing to get the true direction. So, if your compass says West, subtracting 15 degrees would mean you're actually facing slightly more North of West in the true direction.

How to Orient a Map Using a Compass

Going further, you will come to understand how to find your location using a compass and a map. Imagine you're on an adventure but cannot tell exactly where you are, and you happen to have a map and a compass with you. Then all you need to do is follow these simple steps to get your exact location using a map:

16. Using a compass in conjunction with a map makes navigation easier. Source: https://www.pexels.com/photo/compass-lying-on-map-8828457/

Set Up Your Compass with Your Map:

- Hold your compass flat in your hand or lay it flat on the map, which can be on the floor. Find the direction of the North on your map. Most maps have a North arrow to tell you. Now, turn your compass (which is now lying on your map) along with the map so that the direction of north on the compass matches the direction of north on the map. Easy, right?

- Next, find a big landmark nearby. It could be a mountain or a lake, one you can see on both the map and in reality. Now, make sure that the travel arrow is pointing in the direction of the landmark.

- Rotate the edge of the compass (bezel) until the arrow inside (orienting line) lines up perfectly with the North direction on the compass. Now, look at the number on the edge of the compass where the travel arrow points. This number tells you the direction you're facing relative to the North. Keep this number in mind; it will be your bearing.

Triangulation

When your compass is synced with your map, and your bearings have been identified, you can then use the triangulation techniques to know your approximate location on the map. If you're wondering if your approximate location is different from your bearing, you're correct. Your bearing is the direction you're heading or the direction of a landmark from your current position. Your approximate location is your position on a map, which is fact-checked by triangulating your position based on known landmarks or bearings. Here's how to triangulate:

Finding Your Location on the Map:

- Place one corner (edge or the ruler) of the compass's baseplate on the landmark you choose on the map. Now, while keeping the compass in place, rotate the compass (bezel) until the arrow inside (orienting line) is again lined up with the north direction on the compass. Draw a line along the edge of the compass set on your landmark.

- Find another landmark and repeat the steps above. Do this for as many landmarks as you can see. Each time, draw a line on the map starting from the landmark.

- Where the lines you drew intersect is where you are on the map. Congratulations, you just found your location using compass triangulation.

Mastering the compass has never been easier. In this chapter, you've been taken into a process of progressive learning where every new fact you learn about the compass is necessary to understand the next phase of how to use it. The key to mastery is not just exposure to lots of information but consistent practice with what you've just learned. So, make sure you put everything you've learned to the test; that is how your skill gets stronger. For the fun part, try out these games and activities.

Games and Activities

Map-Orienting Relay Race: This will help you practice orienting a map with your friends and family using a compass in a relay race. For this game to be more fun and competitive, you'll need two teams.

Materials Needed:

- Wide open field or area

- Maps of the area (one per team)
- Compasses (one per team)
- Cones or markers to identify start and finish points
- Stopwatch or timer

Instructions:

- Divide participants into teams of 3 or 4 members each.
- Place the start and finish lines far apart, with enough space for both teams to spread out and work on their maps.
- Provide each team with a map and a compass.
- At the signal, the first member of each team runs to the designated map station, where a facilitator hands them a map and a compass.
- The first player uses the compass to orient the map correctly in the North direction.
- Once the map is oriented, the player runs back to tag the next team member, who repeats the process.
- The relay continues until the team members are done orienting the map and the final player crosses the finish line.
- The team with the fastest overall time wins the race.

Note: You can add obstacles or challenges along the relay course to make it more exciting.

Activity 2

The Treasure Hunt Triangulation: To help you practice navigation techniques like triangulation while still searching for some hidden treasures.

Materials Needed:

- A large outdoor space with several landmarks like trees, rocks, and streams.

- Maps of the area with marked coordinates to signify likely areas for the hidden treasures (one per participant or team)

- Compasses (one per participant or team)

- Hidden treasure (optional)

Instructions:

- Mark the coordinates of each treasure location on the maps.

- Participants or teams should be given maps with marked coordinates of the treasure locations.

- Using compasses, participants are to navigate their way to the coordinates marked on their maps.

- Participants will then use triangulation techniques to confirm the treasure's location at each location by identifying nearby landmarks and estimating distances.

- Once they believe they have pinpointed the treasure location, participants begin searching the area to find the hidden treasure.

- The participant or team that finds the most treasures within a set time wins the game.

Note: You can increase the difficulty of this game by using only partial coordinates, which would require everyone to calculate coordinates based on distances and bearings.

Orienting a map with your compass becomes seamless when you apply the triangulation techniques. This chapter has given you the basics of how to set up a compass using a map, how to find your bearings with a compass, and how to correct your compass for declination. You were also provided with games and activities to help enhance your knowledge of the topic. By carrying out these activities, you have a better chance of becoming more and more confident as you use a compass.

Chapter 5: Exploring the Outdoors

Exploring outdoor spaces using compasses can be very exciting. Compasses are your backup when the GPS fails, but they're not the only backups you should consider when exploring. The outdoor space can be quite unfamiliar and unpredictable at times, so you should go with other essential items needed for your journey.

Every tool kit for an adventure is highly dependent on the destination and purpose of the adventure. There are areas where you need a specific kind of compass for accurate readings, and there are those where just any compass goes. For example, some places may have several iron ores beneath the soil, and this may disrupt the readings on your compass, so you'll need a more stable device to navigate in such places.

17. Step into the sunshine, where adventures bloom and the world waits for you to explore! Source: Rademenes777, CC BY-SA 4.0 <https://creativecommons.org/licenses/by-sa/4.0>, via Wikimedia Commons: https://commons.wikimedia.org/wiki/File:Children_playing_on_t he_lawn_outside_the_Regional_Museum_in_Stalowa_Wola.jpg

In this chapter, you will learn important tricks and tips for perfect navigation in the wild. Your safety is the number one priority, so you'll also learn about safety precautions while navigating outdoor spaces and extra tips on how to navigate through certain outdoor spaces.

Safety Precautions When Navigating Outdoors

Learning how to use a compass during navigation helps to prevent you from ever getting lost, but you also need to prioritize your safety during outdoor sports, games, camping, and other adventurous journeys.

Here are safety precautions you should keep in mind:

18. Before exploring, make sure to orient your map so you can determine your location and avoid getting lost. Source: https://unsplash.com/photos/person-holding-white-and-blue-book-KJbo3yYe9lQ

Plan for Your Adventure

Do not venture off into the open field or the wild without deciding on a destination, how to get there, and what the journey needs. Many of the games and activities listed in previous chapters are done in an open area, but when exploring the outdoors further, like taking a short trip or going camping with friends and families, you'll need a few essentials.

Here are tips to help you plan:

- Get a map of that area

- Navigate using your compass

- Check access points to your destination via vehicles and walking

- Check the weather conditions for the day of your adventures

- Ask questions about the area from outdoorsmen (This will be necessary for your first time exploring a new area)

- Don't go alone

- Go during safe hours of the day

Communicate with Trusted Persons

As highlighted in the introduction, there could be unpredictable events during these kind of trips. These are not hidden obstacles you see during a game but real-life events that you should be prepared for. No matter what happens during your journey, always make sure you stay in constant communication with someone from the other end. Here are some key details they should be aware of at all times:

- A timeframe of your expected arrival at the destination

- Copy of the map you will be using

- Possible routes you plan to go through

- Camp and stop points, all marked on the map

- A backup number you can be reached on

- Frequent updates on the status of your trip

- Possible contact numbers of people you're going to be with throughout your trip

Your Adventure Gear

The right gear and tools mean effortless success in your adventures.

Here are some of the best gear to bring along for any trip:

- Compass and Map (Very essential)

- Boots or shoes

- Water-resistant jackets and pants, if possible
- Backpack
- Food and water
- A few extra clothes
- Knife
- First aid kits

If the journey requires you to stop to camp for a break, consider including other camping essentials like:

- Tents, sleeping bags, pillows and pads
- Lanterns, headlamps, flashlights
- Disposable plates, mugs and cutleries
- Drinks and food in a cooler
- Trash bags (to keep your environment clean)
- Portable cooking tools and firewood

Navigation Tips and Tricks

Navigation can be fun and effortless when done the right way using the best tools for a more accurate result. Remember it was mentioned that there are areas that have a high density of iron ore underneath the soil, which will require specific compass types to get a more accurate reading.

Well, here are recommended compasses and maps for easy orientation and efficient navigation in areas like these:

For Your Compass:

- **The Brunton TruArc 15 Compass:** This compass gives accurate readings for navigation in any environment. It's lightweight and durable.

- **The Cammenga Lensatic Compass:** It's perfect for dark or low-lighted areas because it has the tritium illumination effect to glow in low-light areas. If you're looking for a touch of military-grade, this one's for you.

- **The K &R Alpin Compass:** This type is very easy to use and reliable, and it comes in really handy when measuring slopes. It also has an integrated clinometer.

For Your Maps:

- **USGS Topographic Maps:** These show more obvious elevation and contour changes. They also reveal features in terrain areas for better navigation.

- **National Geographic Illustrated Maps:** This map is waterproof and has detailed recreational information for parks and outdoor areas.

Tips for Navigating Different Terrains

19. Navigating the woods can be risky, as you may encounter dangerous animals or come across toxic plants along the way. Source: https://pixabay.com/photos/wood-tree-nature-landscape-forest-3095720/

The Woods:

- Use natural landmarks like unique trees, rock formations, and water bodies to understand your bearings' position.

- Carry biodegradable markers or use natural markers like stones or sticks to mark your trail.

- Whenever possible, stick to known trails—perhaps the ones you marked or those marked by others—to provide a clear route.

- If you need to leave the trail, take a bearing from your starting point and take note of it.

- Learn how to read topographic maps, those that show the elevation and layout of the terrain.

- Make sure you frequently check your compass to ensure you are maintaining the correct direction.

- Wear appropriate footwear and be prepared for a slower journey.

- Be aware of potential hazards like streams, cliffs, and wildlife.

Parks

20. Navigating parks is enjoyable and safer, though it still involves encountering wild animals. Source: Tcc8, CC BY-SA 3.0 <https://creativecommons.org/licenses/by-sa/3.0>, via Wikimedia Commons: https://commons.wikimedia.org/wiki/File:Rhino_san_diego_wild _animal_park.jpg

- You should take note of all entry and exit points.

- You can make use of park maps provided in the visitor's center or by the entrance.

- Use artificial landmarks such as benches, restrooms, playgrounds, and picnic areas as a form of orientation for yourself.

- Take note of the locations and emergency contact points.

- Even in parks, a map and compass could still be useful for navigating less traveled or larger park areas.

- Parks can be very busy with visitors, and this can sometimes make you feel a bit confused. Try to be on guard and alert to avoid getting distracted.

Urban Areas

- Use street maps and apps on your smartphone for a more precise direction.

- Learn the local addresses and numbering system around the area. You should also take note of any street grid patterns to help you find better navigation.

- Some cities have noticeable landmarks or buildings that would be of help in your navigation.

- Familiarize yourself with the local public transportation system, including bus, subway, and train routes.

- Take along your map and compass.

- In urban areas, you should be aware of your surroundings and avoid less populated or poorly lit areas, especially at night.

- Be aware of the time and plan your route to ensure you have enough daylight to return safely.

- Carry a mobile phone or a walkie-talkie for communication.

- If you ever feel lost, do not panic to avoid making poor decisions. Stop and reassess your surroundings calmly.

- Carry a watch and set checkpoints for time management.

- Let someone know your planned route and estimated return time.

Games and Activities

Woods Exploration Challenge: to help you practice basic compass skills and navigation through a wooded area.

Materials Needed:

- Compasses
- Maps of the wooded area
- Flags or markers to assign checkpoints
- Clue cards for each level
- Prizes for the winners

Instructions:

- Place 5 flags or markers at different points in the wooded area.
- Create simple clue cards with bearings and distances to each checkpoint.
- Each participant should be given a compass, a map, and their first clue card.
- The participants should follow the bearings and distances given on the clue card to find each flag.
- At each checkpoint, there should be a token in exchange for the flag they found.
- The first few participants to collect all tokens and return to the start advance to the next level.

Level 2

- Place 5 new flags or markers further apart with a more complex bearing and distance.
- You can add more challenges, like identifying marked trees or landmarks to get a token at the checkpoint.

- The first participant to complete all checkpoints and return to the start wins and is regarded as the new Navigation Master.

The best way to put your skills to work is not just with games but in your day-to-day activities. In this chapter, you learned the importance of using your navigation skills out there and some safety tools to guide you if you ever plan on going camping with friends and families. You've also learned how to use your compass and read your mail in different terrains like urban areas, parks, and forests. By applying the knowledge from this chapter, you're ready to explore the fields with your compass.

Chapter 6: Fun Games and Activities

Understanding the use of a compass is valuable not just for outdoor activities but also for the fun that comes with knowing that your navigation skills are getting more accurate. Learning this skill doesn't have to be technical or done alone; you should make the most of the learning process by engaging friends and families in a fun and creative way.

There are a lot of exciting games and activities to help you improve your compass skills. Some of these activities have been discussed in previous chapters, but you will uncover more in this chapter.

21. Kids can use a compass to play many exciting games, like treasure hunts and orienteering. Source: https://www.pexels.com/photo/a-boy-looking-at-a-compass-while-holding-a-map-8083378/

The good thing about these activities is that there are more ways to play them. You can get creative and use what you have and wherever you are to create the best possible fun time for yourself and others. Enjoy the games discussed below, and don't forget to play safe!

Treasure Hunts Using Compass Directions

Treasure hunts help you get familiar with your compass angles and bearings while hunting and seeking out hidden treasures. The game is simple and can be played by all ages.

This section describes the game for ages 7-13 years of age. The game is very much adjustable for any age group that wishes to play. For older groups, try implementing riddles, quizzes, and other activities to unravel the location of the hidden treasure even after finding the bearings. This will help participants improve and grow their problem-solving skills.

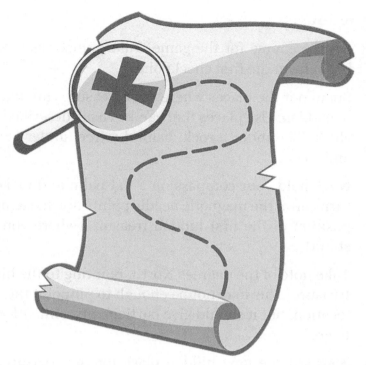

22. Scavenger hunts are always fun but can be more exciting with a compass. Source: https://pixabay.com/vectors/ancient-historic-map-old-parchment-1300292/

Material Needed:

- Different colors of clue cards or boards for each group or individual participant.

- Compass

- Maps (for older ages)

- An open area (park, field, beach, backyard or front lawn)

- Treasures

Instructions:

- Set the course for the game. Take your treasures and begin from the first checkpoint.

- Spam out the places where your treasures are likely to be hidden. Use places that can be easily described with clues, like under a rock, behind a tree, under a chair, and so on.

- Now, hold your compass on a flat palm and make the turns until the magnetic needle points north, facing the position of the first hidden treasure (where you now stand).

- Take note of the degrees North, pointing to the hidden treasure. This may not be enough to pinpoint the exact location, but it should give participants a hint of where to go.

- Spot out the next hidden place for the treasure, and count your steps to that point. Write that down on the clue card as a hint to get to the hidden treasure.

- Children have smaller footsteps, so you should consider that as well so you can make smaller steps.

- Create as many different routes to the treasure as possible to allow the different participants to go at once without taking turns.

Building Obstacle Courses with Compass Directions

Building obstacle courses with a compass is a creative way to teach you how to use and perfect your navigation skills. It teaches you how to read and apply compass directions in a fun and interactive way. You get to build obstacle courses using compass directions, which goes a long way in developing your problem-solving skills, observation, and critical thinking capacity. The most fun part is doing this with your friends, families, or teammates.

Materials:

- Compasses for each group

- A good space out for the game

- Cones, tapes, ropes, or markers for each team to mark obstacles and checkpoints

- Clue cards with compass bearings and distances for navigation

- Stopwatches or timer

- Prizes for winners

Instructions:

- Two teams are provided with a set of materials (e.g., cones, hurdles, tape, etc.).

- Each team is given a compass and a map with a starting point and a finish line.

- The first two teams are to build an obstacle course using compass directions (e.g., "Walk 10 paces North, turn 90 degrees East, walk 5 paces North, and so on.").

- All teammates must work together to navigate the course and make sure it meets the given compass directions.

- Once the course has been built, with obstacles, each team is to test out the course and make adjustments where needed.

- The teams are to then exchange these clues with the other team.

- The team that completes the course in the shortest amount of time wins.

- For younger participants (ages 7-10), you can use simpler compass directions and provide more guidance when and where it's needed.

- For participants ages 11 and above, you can try to add complex directions and obstacles, such as specific landmarks and other features, to the clues.

Creating Scavenger Hunts with Compass Clues

The aim of scavenger hunts is to build your problem-solving skills. They improve your critical thinking and increase your pace at solving navigation problems, like in real-life scenarios. They also teach you how to be a team player and communicate with your friends while having fun and discovering hidden clues. What an exciting and engaging way to develop essential skills while you enjoy an adventure-filled experience!

Materials:

- Compass
- Scavenger hunt list with compass clues
- Map or diagram of the hunt area
- GPS devices or smartphones with GPS apps (this is entirely optional)

Instructions:

- Divide everyone into a team of 2 to 4 persons

- Provide each team with a compass, map, and a scavenger hunt list.

- Create a scavenger hunt list with clues that bear compass directions (for example, "Walk 20 paces North, turn 45 degrees East, find the next clue").

- The next clue should lead them to carry out similar tasks.

- Flood the hunting area with clues and challenges that require the teams to use their compass and problem-solving skills.

- The first team to complete all clues and challenges wins.

Here are examples of clues you can use:

Clue 1: From the starting point, walk 30 paces South. Turn 90 degrees West and find the clue at the base of a tree.

Clue 2: Face North and take 15 paces forward. Turn 180 degrees and find the next clue 5 paces away.

Clue 3: Use your compass to find the direction of the sun. Walk 20 paces in that direction and find the clue.

Tips For the Hunt

- Add GPS coordinates or QR codes to clues to make them extra challenging.

- You can make it a themed scavenger hunt, using themes such as nature, literature, and history to make it more engaging.

Interactive Group Activities to Enhance Navigation Skills

Compass Relay Race: To help you practice basic compass skills using teamwork in a fun, competitive relay race.

Materials:

- Compasses (one for each team)
- Cones or markers to mark checkpoints
- Clue cards with compass bearing and hints for the game
- Tokens or flags at each checkpoint

Instructions:

- Choose a large open area for the game.
- Set up several checkpoints in the area.
- Place a token or a flag at each checkpoint.
- Assign everyone into teams of 2 to 4.
- Each team gets a compass and a set of instructions for the first leg of the race.
- The first member of the team starts at the first checkpoint using the compass to get the bearing on the clue card.
- Upon reaching the next checkpoint, the first member collects the token and hands the compass to the next team member.
- The second member continues to the next checkpoint using the new set of bearings and distances.

- The race continues with each team member navigating one leg of the course.

- The first team to collect all tokens and reach the final checkpoint wins.

Orienteering Challenge: To help you practice advanced navigation techniques by using a compass with a map and triangulation techniques through a mapped-out orienteering area.

Materials:

- Compasses (one per team)

- Detailed maps of the area with checkpoints marked

- Control cards for recording checkpoints

- Flags or markers at each checkpoint

- Lunches or pens for marking control cards

Introduction:

- Place flags or markers at various checkpoints around the area.

- Each checkpoint should be marked on the map and have a unique code or punch.

- Divide players into groups of 3 or 4 and hand them a compass, map, and control card.

- They all begin at the start point and use their maps and compasses to navigate to each checkpoint in the correct order.

- Whenever a team gets to a checkpoint, they mark their control card with the unique code or punch.

- The first group to navigate through all checkpoints and return with a completed control card wins.

23. Kids walk in a straight line, using the compass to ensure they are on the correct path. Source: https://www.pexels.com/photo/group-of-children-walking-on-a-pathway-9292928/

Most compass games and activities are more effective outdoors than they are indoors. These games are to prepare you for a world of unexplored adventure. Using these outdoor games would give you a real-life notion in testing your newly acquired navigation skills. Don't forget to get creative with the games and better improve them to suit the age group of participants, the environment, and the materials available to play. Keep a keen eye on your environment, and stay safe.

Chapter 7: Real-Life Applications

There was once a time when the only reliable means of navigation was reading the direction of the sun and the stars. Still, that time evolved, and so did the methods of finding direction.

Before the compass was invented, people learned how to make magnetic needles. They would place these needles on pieces of wood or cork and float them on water to figure out which way was north or south. This was because the magnetic needle always pointed in the Northern direction. As much as the navigation systems have evolved, the earth's magnetic pole has not, so the compass will forever be useful in real-life applications. The compass will always be a handy and essential requirement to tackle certain navigation problems.

24. Compasses help you find your way in everyday adventures! Source: https://www.pexels.com/photo/little-girls-looking-at-a-compass-8082902/

There are careers, professions, and hobbies that depend solely on this small tool to carry out usual tasks, and these you'll discover in this chapter.

How Compass Skills are Useful in Everyday Life

How valuable this tool is depends on your understanding of how to use it. If you've ever been in a situation where your only source of bearing was a map, you may understand the value of knowing how to read a compass with a map and always having one with you.

Professions like sailing, astronomy, piloting, archaeology, and the like, which are always about going places and exploring new locations, find this skill very essential. Having a skill means making a difference, and in doing so, you will have to effectively and readily put to work your knowledge about something. It means you can only claim to have a skill when you can confidently use it in real-life situations to make a difference. Take a look at these real-life scenarios:

- Going hiking with friends

- Going on an excursion to a place you've never been

- On a holiday with your family

- Going camping with friends, schoolmates, or family

- On a tour in a different environment or country

- Moving to a new house

- Finding your way in a forest

- Going fishing with your parents or friends

- Going treasure hunting

- Finding your way to an event

It's an endless list. In all these cases, you should keep your GPS close and your compass closer.

Professions and Hobbies Where Navigation Skills Are Crucial

It's not news to you that people are always moving. Have you ever wondered why you are never alone on your road to school or the grocery shop? Every time you set out to a destination, there are people in every direction you turn. Every day, millions of people are traveling via airplanes, trains, cars, buses, bicycles, tricycles, walking, and running everywhere in the world. However, only a few of these people know or have learned how to use the compass and the map. Here are examples of professions and hobbies where compass navigation skills cannot be unexplored:

Geologists

It would amaze you to know that the world map was actually drawn using a compass. Scientists were only able to measure its surface, width, and length by traveling around the world several times to measure and take notes of distances and locations. With the compass, a geologist can locate and map land and area formations, survey areas, and conduct field research.

25. With the compass, a geologist can locate and map land and area formations, survey areas, and conduct field research. Source: https://www.pexels.com/photo/view-of-rock-formation-258118/

Foresters

These guys plant and remove trees from the ground. Eventually, they are sold to meet consumer demands for beautiful furniture, house structures, papers, and lots more. They navigate through different forests using a compass and a map.

Surveyors

These professionals are the reason why countries around the world have land mass. Without surveyors, there would be no borders or property boundaries. They also do a lot more and are very related to geologists. They conduct topographic surveys and create accurate maps.

Pilots / Sailors

These professionals need exceptional navigation skills to chart out flight sea plans, navigate through airspace and water, and ensure that there are safe landing spaces.

These are a few of the countless professions that need navigation skills to deliver their services better. Some others include archaeologists, astronomers, urban planners, and so on. Outside the professional game, a lot of hobbies also require navigation skills Like;

Mountain Climbing

Going on a short mountain trip would mean walking your way there. So, this hobby definitely requires navigation skills to locate routes and shortcuts, avoid hazards, and reach your destination safely.

Hiking

When hiking, you want to avoid getting lost on those trails, so you use the compass to stay on track or find your track. Other hobbies that involve the use of compass navigation are sailing, adventure racing, diving, treasure hunting, and lots more.

Inspiring Stories of Adventurers and Explorers Who Relied on Compass Navigation

There are countless inspiring stories of people who went from zero compass skills to having their first experiences, which played a great role in the success of their journey. Here are some inspiring stories you can learn from:

26. Many adventurers and explorers have made remarkable discoveries and overcome immense challenges by relying on their compass navigation skills. Source: https://www.pexels.com/photo/compass-and-a-toy-boat-on-a-map-8828579/

1. Identical twin sisters, Jennifer and Amiee Roberge, are avid fitness enthusiasts. They took the CanoeSki map and compass course to prepare them for their adventure on the reality TV show "Mantracker." This was their first outdoor experience, and luckily, they learned really great navigation skills, including reading maps and using the compass. This skill gave them the confidence they needed to navigate through the wilderness, and they gave credit to Cliff's course for their success. They gave a review saying, "Thanks, Cliff, for getting us prepared. You're an upstanding gentleman who knows his stuff!"

2. Colin Jolly is a recreation coordinator and canoe instructor. He also took the CanoeSki map and

compass course to enhance his outdoor skills. He found the course to be very beneficial, as it gave him the opportunity to learn how to read a map and use the compass effectively. The course's split format, with both classroom and field practice, was perfect for Colin. He highly recommended the course, saying, "I believe anyone involved in outdoor activities should take this course."

3. Vicki Cirkvencic is a Saskatoon firefighter and sea kayaking instructor. She took the initiative to enhance her skills by learning how to use a compass and a map. After taking this bold step, she appreciated the opportunity to learn land navigation techniques, which complemented her sea kayaking experience.

4. John Rooney, an avid backpacker, seized the opportunity to gain the skills and confidence to navigate in the backcountry. It helped him in a professional, informative, fun, and knowledgeable way. John appreciated the opportunity to practice his new skills in an orienteering exercise and was able to apply them on his subsequent backpacking trips.

The skill of having a compass sense can be applied in many fields of life, be it games, professions, hobbies, or other spheres. This is one skill that will never become obsolete even as the world evolves. So, you're doing the right thing, learning to grow your skill in using the compass.

Chapter 8: Further Resources

The most vital part of any learning experience is applying all you understand in real-life situations and taking the time to go over them till you've perfected every angle. The compass, like every other tool, can be more easily wielded with time and more practice. You can showcase your newly formed skill with the games created for you in every chapter, and then, to solidify your compass experience, you can apply that knowledge to real outdoor activities. In this chapter, you'll be given a recap on the key compass navigation concept and a final thought on the importance of navigation and exploration in the modern world.

27. Learning to navigate and explore is like having a magical map that guides us to new adventures, and helps us discover amazing places
Source: https://unsplash.com/photos/two-children-standing-near-cliff-watching-on-ocean-at-daytime-XRcEsQKTWGk

Key Compass Navigation Concepts

As an essential navigation tool, the compass has been efficient for centuries and even in the present day. Its abilities for navigation, irrespective of your location, or the weather conditions, have made it a relevant tool in many fields of work, even today. As you learned in previous chapters, the compass has a magnetic needle that points you to the earth's magnetic pole. This magnetic needle is always positioned to the North, but further down the line, you discover that the earth has two North- the magnetic North and the true North. The true North is where the earth's north pole is positioned. To find your true North on the compass before navigation, you have to adjust the compass' magnetic North to align with the true North. This is what you call the declination of a compass.

After finding your true North, the next step would be to find your bearing. Your bearing is the degree of your position on the map to your destination or the nearest landmark. The landmark should be something you can spot both on the map and in real time. If you don't know what your exact bearing is on the map, you can find that through what is called triangulation. All of these concepts have been explained in previous chapters. The compass will play a huge role for you in locations and positions where your GPS is likely to malfunction. This is why it's mostly used in surveys, aircraft, ships, mountains, hiking, and so on.

Continue Practicing and Honing Your Compass Skills

It's been an amazing journey learning about the methods of navigating with a compass. If there's one thing you need to remember constantly, it's that the key to becoming an expert in the field of navigation is through consistent practice. Every time you use your compass to explore new places, you're building skills that will stay with you for life. Here are a few tips to help you:

- **Stay Curious:** You should keep asking questions and exploring new ways to use your compass. The more curious you are, the more you'll discover about the world around you.

- **Frequent Practice:** Set aside some time each week or each day to practice your navigation skills. Whether it's a short walk in the park or a weekend hike in the woods, every bit of practice would go a long way.

- **Take on Challenges:** Keep trying out new challenges. New challenges and activities will help push you beyond your limits. The more you challenge yourself, the more confident and skilled you'll become.

- **Don't Keep Your Knowledge to Yourself; Share It with Others:** This is one secret that people don't often talk about. The more you share your knowledge, the more it becomes a constant play in your mind, and the faster you get to the expertise stage.

- **Encourage Yourself:** Celebrate every little improvement. It's not an easy task to learn the skills of a compass, so don't be too hard on yourself. Every time you successfully navigate to a new place or complete a challenge, take a moment to celebrate your achievements. You're doing an awesome job.

- **Stay Safe:** Always ensure you're well prepared before embarking on any adventure, and stay safe while exploring. Use your skills wisely and never take unnecessary risks.

Importance of Navigation and Exploration in the Modern World

The evolution of navigation has definitely transformed how you can explore the world, and this has helped in many discoveries globally. With the help of the modernized compass, adventurers have embarked on journeys with so much confidence, knowing that this tool is sufficient to direct them to unfamiliar territories with ease.

Can you imagine how this will affect the way you live?

You no longer have to guess what a place looks like through a map or in pictures; you can actually explore it and see for yourself. This brings a form of healing and builds a mindset that you can conquer and get anywhere you set your heart and your mind to.

Prior to this chapter, you discovered that the compass has now evolved into other forms of navigation, such as your GPS. This can be effective during travels, exploration, and interaction with your world at large. The GPS is just one of the many modernized forms of compass today. You also have other applications that assist you during some of your explorations and enhance your ability to navigate through both familiar and unfamiliar terrains.

The evolution of the GPS compass has also created a possibility for what is called "geo-location." You can apply this to either your video games or location-based services. Location-based services allow the applications in your devices or your device itself to use your location to search out services or contents that are relevant to you from that location. This is just a more advanced way to put your compass skills to work. However, the compass itself still stands to be more effective in navigating terrains. You can do so much during your trips when you hone your navigation skills. To become a master wielder of the compass, you have to master the basics and build up from there. More practice means more confidence, even when you're out alone during your adventures.

Conclusion

Did you have fun learning about compasses? They are fascinating, aren't they? These small tools aren't just for playing. They can also save people's lives. Learning how to use them is an important skill that will help you now and in the future.

The book started by explaining compasses and their role in navigation. It then covered compass parts, how they work, and their importance in outdoor activities.

Understanding the four directions is key to using a compass. You also found out about bearing and degrees. The fun exercises taught you how to use compasses in navigation.

Compasses can be used in many things. You discovered how to use them to read maps and triangulate.

Safety is important when using a compass outside. The book gave safety tips for exploring parks, woods, and other places.

The exciting games and activities you practiced helped you understand compass directions and clues and improved your navigation skills.

You also learned how compasses can be used daily and which hobbies use navigation skills.

Do you know what you want to be when you grow up? You can choose a job where you can use a compass every day.

You discovered inspiring stories of explorers and adventurers who used a compass in navigation.

Now that you have learned about compasses, you can go outside and explore.

Thank you for reading this book. Did you enjoy it? Please remember to leave a review.

Key Takeaways

- Compasses are important for outdoor navigation.
- You can't use a compass without understanding the four directions.
- Maps can be oriented with a compass.
- You should be careful when using compasses outdoors.
- Practicing games and activities will improve your navigation skills.
- You can find your dream job where you can use a compass every day.

References

A beginners guide to using a compass. (n.d.). Org.uk. https://www.ramblers.org.uk/go-walking-hub/beginners-guide-using-compass

Compass types - different types of compasses. (n.d.). Historyofcompass.com. http://www.historyofcompass.com/compass-facts/compass-types/

No title. (n.d.). Johnsonoutdoors.com. https://eurekacamping.johnsonoutdoors.com/us/blog/compass-parts-know-your-instrument

(N.d.). Rei.com. https://www.rei.com/learn/expert-advice/navigation-basics.html

Camping Zest. (2021, December 2). *How to use a compass: For kids.* Camping Zest. https://campingzest.com/how-to-use-a-compass-for-kids/

No title. (n.d.-a). Com.Ng. https://www.twinkl.com.ng/teaching-wiki/compass

No title. (n.d.-b). Study.com. https://study.com/academy/lesson/history-of-the-compass-lesson-for-kids.html

A beginners guide to using a compass. (n.d.). Org.uk. https://www.ramblers.org.uk/go-walking-hub/beginners-guide-using-compass

No title. (n.d.). Study.com. https://study.com/academy/lesson/cardinal-intermediate-directions-definition-meaning.html

Qiu, L. (2023, May 24). *Learn how to use a compass and never get lost again.* Backpacker. https://www.backpacker.com/skills/navigation/how-to-use-a-compass/?scope=anon

(N.d.). Rei.com. https://www.rei.com/learn/expert-advice/navigation-basics.html

Learning magnetic compass. (n.d.). Compassdude.com. http://www.compassdude.com/compass-skills.php

Konrad. (2023). Master the wilderness: The ultimate guide to advanced compass navigation – 2024. https://mendooutdoors.com/master-the-wilderness-the-ultimate-guide-to-advanced-compass-navigation/

Mountain run (en-GB). (n.d.). Mountainrun.co.uk. https://mountainrun.co.uk/news/advanced-navigation-beyond-the-intermediate-basics

(N.d.). Rei.com. https://www.rei.com/learn/expert-advice/navigation-basics.html

Vigilant Survival. (2023, April 19). Lost in the Woods? No problem! How to navigate with a compass and map. Medium. https://medium.com/@todd_3917/lost-in-the-woods-no-problem-how-to-navigate-with-a-compass-and-map-2e08ec690d10

Kendall, A. (2015, June 9). How NOT to get lost in the woods: Navigation 5 Top Tips. Wilderness Scotland. https://www.wildernessscotland.com/blog/how-not-to-get-lost-in-the-woods-navigation-5-top-tips/

How to stay safe outdoors & recreate responsibly. (n.d.). Stanley 1913 https://www.stanley1913.com/blogs/how-to-guides/how-to-stay-safe-outdoors-and-recreate-responsibly

Robinson, M. (2019, August 14). Outdoor lesson idea. Learning through Landscapes. https://ltl.org.uk/resources/compass-treasure-hunt/

Mom, S. (2022, April 16). Orienteering scavenger hunt. Scouter Mom. https://scoutermom.com/21794/orienteering-scavenger-hunt/

Compass treasure hunt. (2017, October 12). Eartheasy Guides & Articles; Eartheasy. https://learn.eartheasy.com/guides/compass-treasure-hunt/

No title. (n.d.). Johnsonoutdoors.com. https://eurekacamping.johnsonoutdoors.com/us/blog/3-compass-games-teach-kids-use-compass

Using a compass. (n.d.). Nrcan.Gc.Ca. https://geomag.nrcan.gc.ca/mag_fld/compass-en.php

Map & compass stories. (n.d.). CanoeSki Discovery Company. https://www.canoeski.com/map-compass-stories/

Hanke, W. (2010, November 29). Map and compass skills. Missouri Float Trips. https://www.floatmissouri.com/map-and-compass-skills/

What is a compass' Mysteries: Expert Insights ». (n.d.). Design Match https://www.designmatch.io/vocabulary/what-is-a-compass/

McCafferty/Field, K., & Stream. (2017, July 7). Five map and compass skills every outdoorsman should master. Popular Science. https://www.popsci.com/five-map-and-compass-skills-every-outdoorsman-should-master/

Importance of exploration. (2018, January 30). Breaking the Cycle – Education. https://www.breakingthecycle.education/about/importance-of-exploration/

Anand, S. (2024, March 20). Exploring the benefits of navigation technology. Linkedin.com. https://www.linkedin.com/pulse/exploring-benefits-navigation-technology-saurabh-anand-uwsce

Navigation compass: Definition, diagram, how to use it, uses. (2023, April 27). Testbook. https://testbook.com/physics/navigation-compass

Made in the USA
Las Vegas, NV
21 December 2024

14953005R00046